OLD CARS

Sally Morgan

FRANKLIN WATTS
LONDON•SYDNEY

First published in 2006 by
Franklin Watts
338 Euston Road,
London NW1 3BH

Franklin Watts Australia
Hachette Children's Books
Level 17/207 Kent Street,
Sydney NSW 2000

Produced for Franklin Watts by White-Thomson Publishing Ltd
210 High Street,
Lewes BN7 2NH

Editor: Rachel Minay
Designer: Brenda Cole
Picture research: Morgan Interactive Ltd
Consultant: Graham Williams

Picture credits:
The publishers would like to thank the following for reproducing these photographs:
Alamy 24 (Chuck Pefley); Corbis 9 (Alain Denize/Sygma), 18 (Peter Yates);
Digitalvision front cover main image; Ecoscene front cover top right (Ian Harwood),
6 (Jon Bower), 7 (Angela Hampton), 8 (Andrew Brown), 10 (Alex Bartel), 11
(Rosemary Greenwood), 12 (Anthony Cooper), 13 (Angela Hampton), 15 (Vicki
Coombs), 16 (Tony Page), 17 (Mark Tweedie), 19 (Ceanne Jensen), 20 (Paul
Kennedy), 21 (Guy Stubbs), 22 (Vicki Coombs), 23 (Stephen Coyne) 25 (Sally
Morgan), 26 (Adrian Morgan), 27 (Mike Maidment); Recyclenow.com front cover
bottom right.

Every attempt has been made to clear copyright. Should there be
any inadvertent omission please apply to the publisher for rectification.

British Library Cataloguing in Publication Data
A CIP catalogue record for this book
is available from the British Library.

ISBN-10: 0 7496 6435 5   J 363.728
ISBN-13: 978 0 7496 6435 0   1773446

Dewey classification: 363.72'88

Printed in China

Contents

Millions of cars

There are hundreds of millions of cars in the world. Each year the number goes up as millions more cars are manufactured.

Cars around the world

The number of cars is rapidly increasing in countries such as China and India. As these countries become more developed, people can afford to buy cars. In countries such as the UK, USA, Germany and Australia, owning a car is commonplace and many families have two or even three cars.

Not only do cars pollute the air, they cause traffic jams in cities.

Burning fuel

Cars need fuel and this fuel comes from oil. Oil is a type of fossil fuel and it is formed underground over millions of years from the remains of plants and animals. However, oil supplies are running out. Oil is unsustainable and it is being used up much faster than new oil is being made.

The car engine produces gases when the fuel is burnt. These include carbon dioxide and nitrogen oxides. They can cause air pollution, such as acid rain and smog. Acid rain damages trees and buildings around the world. Carbon dioxide is a greenhouse gas that traps heat in the Earth's atmosphere. It contributes to global warming.

People depend on cars to get about in their daily lives, for example when shopping or travelling to work or school. The use of public transport has declined in recent years.

It's my world!

How many cars does your family own? Can you work out how many kilometres your family travels in a car each week? How could you cut down on the number of kilometres? Could you use public transport for some journeys?

Getting rid of old cars

One of the biggest problems today is disposing of all the old cars when they come to the end of their lives. Lots of resources were used to make these cars and so it is important that as much as possible is recycled.

In this book you will read about the different materials that are used to build cars and how a car can be taken to pieces and recycled at the end of its life.

Car parts

A car is a complex piece of machinery. A typical family car is made up of about 15,000 separate parts. These are made from many different raw materials.

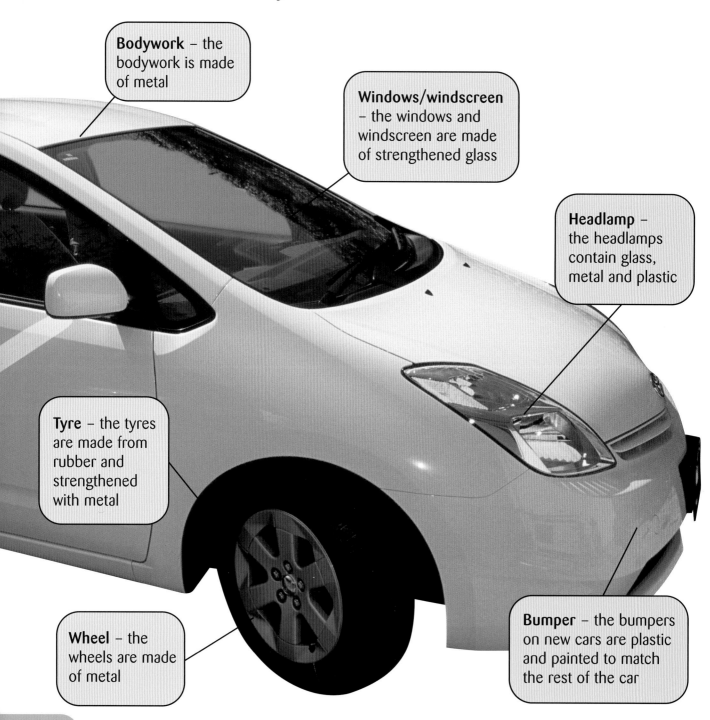

Bodywork – the bodywork is made of metal

Windows/windscreen – the windows and windscreen are made of strengthened glass

Headlamp – the headlamps contain glass, metal and plastic

Tyre – the tyres are made from rubber and strengthened with metal

Wheel – the wheels are made of metal

Bumper – the bumpers on new cars are plastic and painted to match the rest of the car

Raw materials

Car manufacture requires iron, steel, aluminium, zinc, lead, copper, platinum and a range of other materials such as glass and plastic. The body of a car is made up of an underbody, or floorpan, sides and a roof. It has to be strong enough to protect the people inside so it is made from a metal such as steel. The metal is covered in many layers of paint and a top layer of wax to protect the paint. The inside of the bodywork is covered with plastics and fabric. The seats are made from foam and covered with fabric or leather.

Did you know...?

Every second a new car is produced somewhere in the world and more than 48 million new cars are made each year. Millions of tonnes of materials such as steel and plastic are needed to make these cars.

A number of materials are used inside a car. This car's dashboard is made up of plastic with dials of glass and metal, while the seats and steering wheel are covered in leather.

Engine and exhaust

A car's engine and exhaust pipe are made from a metal such as steel or aluminium. When the fuel burns inside the engine it produces hot gases that expand rapidly and push on the piston. This causes the wheels to turn. The gases leave the engine via the exhaust. There is also a fuel tank and pipes to supply the engine with fuel. The engine is connected to a gearbox, clutch and braking system. Extensive wiring controls the engine, lights and alarm system. The wiring is covered in a protective plastic sleeve.

In addition, there are windows made from glass and lots of pieces of plastic such as the bumpers, wheel arches and door handles.

A car's life

Cars are made in factories. A modern factory has a long assembly line where the frame of the car is moved on a conveyor belt past robots and workers who add parts to the car.

Robots on either side of the conveyor belt are welding together the grey steel panels that make up the body of the car. The doors will be fitted next and then the whole car sprayed with paint.

Did you know...?

It is estimated that about 27 tonnes of waste are produced during the extraction of the raw materials that are needed to make one car.

Preparing the bodywork

In the press shop, a huge sheet of metal is cut up into shapes that make the car body. Robots build the floorpan of the car, leaving spaces for the wheel arches and boot wells. Then the sides and roof are welded into place. Doors are made and attached to the body. Once the bodywork is complete, lasers check the surface for the smallest fault. The car is cleaned, rinsed and moved to the paint shop where paint is sprayed over the body with a finishing layer of wax.

Fitting out the inside

The next stage is to fit out the inside of the car. First the wiring is put in place, then the carpets are laid, followed by the seats and other fittings. The windscreen and windows are glued into place. Finally, the engine, clutch and gearbox are lowered into position. The fuel tank is positioned towards the back of the car. Once the engine is in place, the suspension, steering, radiator and battery are added, and then the wheels and tyres. Finally, water, antifreeze, oil and fuel are added so the car engine can be turned on and tested. Now it is ready to be transported to the dealers who sell the cars.

It's my world!

Have a close look at your family's car. How many different materials have been used on the exterior bodywork? How many other materials have been used to make the seats and to line the interior of the car?

Too many vehicles are abandoned in the countryside at the end of their lives rather than being disposed of properly.

Repair or scrap?

A modern car has a lifespan of about 10–15 years. It can be repaired when it goes wrong and parts of the body can be replaced if they are damaged in accidents. However, cars are expensive to repair so an older car is often scrapped if it has been in a serious accident or if the engine needs replacing. Many countries have strict rules controlling the disposal of cars. Often the owner has to pay to have a car scrapped.

Reduce, reuse and recycle

More cars mean that more of the world's resources are being used up in their manufacture. More cars mean that more fuel is burnt and there is more congestion on the roads. Somehow the number of cars on the roads has to be reduced. This can be achieved by reducing, reusing and recycling.

Reducing the number of cars

One way to solve the problem of disposing of old cars is to make fewer cars in the first place. A good public transport system means people can get around without having to buy a car. People could use trains, buses or trams rather than cars. Many cars on the road are occupied by just one person. If more people shared cars there would be fewer cars on the road.

School buses, such as this one in the USA, transport large numbers of pupils to and from school and so fewer individual journeys are made by car.

Reusing cars

An older car can cost a lot of money to repair and this means that cars are scrapped rather than repaired. Cheaper repairs would help to make the car last longer. Car designers could help. They could design the car in a way to make sure that the engine and other parts are easy to access for repair. The bodywork should be easy to remove and replace. Much of a car repair bill is not the cost of spare parts but the cost of the labour to carry out the repair. Often the engine has to be removed to replace a part and this takes a lot of time. If more thought was put into car engine design these costs could be reduced.

It's my world!

Think before you get in a car. Is the journey necessary? Could you walk or cycle instead? Could you get a bus, tram or train? If more people used public transport, there would be fewer cars on the roads and less congestion in towns and cities. Walking and cycling are the most environmentally friendly options, as no fuel is needed.

Recycling cars

Eventually a car reaches the end of its life and it has to be scrapped. It is important that as much of the car as possible is recycled.

These cars are called end-of-life vehicles. In the UK, as many as 2.2 million vehicles are scrapped each year, while in the USA, the total is about 10 million. A modern car is designed so that it can be taken apart and recycled more easily than in the past. In the European Union, there are laws that make the car manufacturer responsible for the disposal of end-of-life vehicles.

This family is using bicycles to get around the town they live in rather than driving in a car.

Scrapyards

When a car reaches the end of its life it has to be scrapped. Most cars and other vehicles are taken to scrapyards, where the various parts are removed and reused wherever possible.

Removing engines

First, the car engine is checked to see if it can be resold for use in another car. The car engine is made from metal so it is valuable. If it cannot be reused, it can be sold as an 'engine core' to businesses that specialise in rebuilding engines.

Identify type of car	
Remove battery	Recycle metals and plastics
Remove tyres and the lead weights from the wheel rims	Recycle or reuse tyres Recycle lead weights
Drain out all liquids such as fuel, coolants, brake fluid, engine oil	Recycle as many fluids as possible and safely dispose of the rest
Remove oil filter, catalytic converter from exhaust and other parts from engine	Burn old filters Recycle catalytic converter
Remove air bags, seats, seat belts, carpeting and other items that can be reused	
Engine removed; remains of car (mostly bodywork) crushed and shredded	Engine and shredded metal recycled Any remains disposed of safely

Saving fluids

The car engine contains a range of fluids that have to be drained out, for example oil, antifreeze and brake oil. The oil is collected, filtered to remove dirt and recycled. The coolant has to be pumped out of the car's air conditioning units. Antifreeze is found in the radiator, where it stops water from freezing.

It is drained, filtered and checked for efficiency. It has to be able to protect the radiator down to temperatures of -28 ˚C/-20 ˚F. If it is of good enough quality, it is put into containers and resold. Any petrol or diesel in the fuel tank is removed and usually used in the vehicles owned by the scrapyard.

These shelves are stacked with spare parts taken from scrapped cars. They are sorted according to the type and model of car from which they were taken.

Did you know...?

Older cars have freon as the coolant in their air conditioning unit. This chemical is a type of CFC (chloro-fluorocarbon) that is harmful to the ozone layer. The freon has to be drained out carefully to make sure that it does not escape into the atmosphere.

Second-hand parts

The tyres are removed and either sold or recycled (see page 21). Lots of other parts can be removed from the car, such as seats, a radio, light bulbs, speakers, windscreen washers, carpets and mats. People can buy these second-hand parts for their own cars. If parts of the bodywork – for example the doors and bonnet – are in good condition, they may also be removed and sold with the other spare parts. Finally, the remains of the car, which is mostly the bodywork, are crushed and recycled – and perhaps used to make other cars.

Metal recycling

The bodywork of a car is usually made of metal, along with the engine and other parts such as the exhaust. Metals are valuable materials and they can be recycled over and over again without any loss of quality.

Steel and aluminium

Cars contain a lot of steel and aluminium in the bodywork and the engine. The bodywork is made of thin metal so that it is strong but does not weigh too much. Aluminium is used in cars because it is a lighter metal than steel. A car engine made from aluminium rather than steel weighs much less and so the car uses less fuel. The main part of the engine is often made from recycled aluminium foil. Scrap aluminium is heated until it melts. The molten metal is poured into moulds to make ingots (large blocks of pure metal) and sold to car manufacturers.

Molten aluminium is a red hot liquid. Here it is being poured into moulds.

Extracting metal

It is cheaper and more efficient to recycle metals as only a few metals can be taken straight from the ground, such as gold. Most metals occur in the form of a metal ore. The ores are dug from the ground in mines or quarries. This creates a lot of waste in the form of soil and rock. Habitats are lost and the mining operation causes harmful pollution.

The ore is crushed and then transported to the refinery. Often this is on the other side of the world. Finally the ore is processed so that the metal comes out and can be used. This uses lots of energy and creates yet more pollution.

The metal from scrapped cars is shredded and then sent to a factory for melting down.

Did you know...?

Modern cars contain a catalytic converter within the exhaust system. It absorbs harmful gases so that the car produces less air pollution. The catalytic converter is a stainless steel tube containing metals such as platinum, rhodium or palladium. These are valuable metals so it is well worth recycling them.

Melting and recycling

Metals are easy to recycle. First, they are sorted into types. Steel can be separated from aluminium by using a magnet. Then, they are simply heated until they melt. They can be rolled or shaped into a new object. Although energy is needed to melt the metal, this is far less than the energy required to extract and transport the ore. Metals can be recycled over and over again without losing any of their properties.

17

Plastics

Over the last 30 years the plastic content of an average vehicle has more than tripled, from about 32 kg in 1970 to 114 kg today. That's about 11% of a car. Plastic parts include the bumpers, the car interior and mats.

Lightweight plastics

Plastics are lighter than many alternative materials. For example, a part made from plastic weighs half that of the same part made in steel. This means that a car with a high plastic content is much lighter in weight but just as strong. A lighter car does not use so much fuel. For example, a reduction in car weight of 300 kg saves about 1,000 litres of fuel during the average life of a car.

Did you know...?

Most modern cars have bumpers painted the same colour as the body. This causes problems during recycling, as the paint has to be removed before the plastic can be recycled and this is pushing up the cost. Manufacturers are looking for ways of removing the paint cheaply.

Long-lasting plastics

Plastics have other valuable properties. They do not rust like steel – so can be used on the outside of the car – and they do not need to be covered by a protective layer of paint. Plastic parts last a long time and they do not scratch or dent as easily as metal. They are also cheaper to make. Plastics can be made into shapes that would be impossible with metals and have allowed car designers to produce exciting car designs.

Car designers have to make sure that the plastic parts of a car can be easily removed and recycled.

This pile of plastic waste is waiting to be recycled. Plastics are sorted, cleaned and then broken up into small flakes, which can be poured into large sacks and taken to factories that make plastics.

Recycling plastic

The higher plastic content of a modern car means it is important to reuse or recycle as much as possible at the end of a car's life. The various parts are removed, sorted into types of plastic and either sold as second-hand replacement parts or sent to plastic recycling companies to be processed. One problem with removing and sorting all the plastics is the cost. Often it can cost more to remove, identify and process the plastic than it would to buy new.

Car manufacturers are also using more recycled plastic to make new plastic parts. Soft drinks bottles are being recycled into engine parts while old carpeting made of nylon (a synthetic fabric made from oil) is being recycled into parts for the fan in the engine. Ford, one of the world's largest car manufacturers, wants its suppliers to make plastic car parts with at least 25% recycled plastic content.

Problem tyres

A tyre is made mostly from rubber, steel and textiles such as cotton. Tyres have to be replaced when they wear down or get punctured. When a tyre comes to the end of its life, it can be reused, recycled, buried in a landfill or burnt.

Old tyres have just been dumped on this beach in the USA. This is a waste of resources as the materials in a tyre are valuable and could be reused or recycled.

Burning tyres

Tyres can be burnt but they produce a mass of black smoke. If tyres have to be burnt, the best place is in an incinerator, where the pollution can be controlled and the heat used to generate electricity. Some cement manufacturers burn tyres instead of coal as a source of heat in the kilns where cement is made. This reduces the amount of coal that has to be used.

Did you know...?

In the USA, about 290 million tyres were scrapped in 2003 alone. About 80% of these tyres were reused or recycled, but the rest ended up in landfills or were dumped in the countryside. In the UK, about 50 million tyres are scrapped each year, most of which are reused or recycled.

Reusing tyres

Tyres can be put to new uses. For example, they can be used as plant containers in the garden or swings in a playground. They are even used to build new coral reefs along some tropical coasts. Tyres in good condition can be made into retreads. The old tread is removed and a new tread stuck on in its place. Retreading allows the tyre to be used for longer and avoids having to buy a new tyre. Retreads are cheap to buy but they are not as safe as new tyres. Cars fitted with retreads cannot be driven at high speeds.

These men in South Africa are cutting up old tyres and painting them to use as decorative features in a garden.

Recycling tyres

The rubber of a tyre can be cut up to make mats and shoe soles. It can be shredded into crumbs and used to make flooring, playground and road surfaces, carpet underlay and noise insulation, as well as new tyres. Now that there are so many uses for an old tyre, tyres have become more valuable and fewer are thrown away.

It's my world!

Look out for things made using old tyres. For example, an old tyre can be used to make a plant container or the seat of a swing. See if the surface of your local playground is made from rubber. Some boots are also made from recycled rubber.

Batteries

Cars need a battery to start the engine. A typical car battery is a 12 V lead-acid battery, which consists of a plastic container containing several pieces of lead surrounded by an acid solution. There are two metal knobs on the top, which are connected to wires from the engine.

Starting the engine

A battery is a store of electricity. When the key is turned in the ignition, the battery delivers a short burst of power to the starter motor and this starts the engine. Each time this happens the battery loses some of its electrical store but it is recharged when the car engine is running. Eventually the battery goes flat and it has to be replaced.

Recycling batteries

Most car batteries are recycled. Old batteries are swapped for new ones at garages and the garages send the old ones for recycling. During the recycling process, the acid is drained away and the battery is hammered into pieces. To separate the different materials, the bits are dropped into a large container of liquid, where the plastic bits float and the heavy lead bits sink. Often the lead and plastic in a lead-acid battery has been recycled many times. A typical lead-acid battery contains 60–80% recycled lead and plastic.

These batteries have been taken from scrapped cars. If they are not sold they will be sent for recycling.

Dry batteries

The lead-acid battery in a car is very different to the small alkaline batteries used in electrical goods such as toys and personal stereos. However, alkaline batteries also contain metals that can be recycled. Some alkaline batteries can be recharged and used again but most have to be thrown away when they are flat. These should be taken to battery recycling points where they can be collected and the parts recycled.

Somebody has dumped a pile of car batteries and tyres in the countryside. The contents of the car batteries could pollute the ground and harm wildlife.

Glass recycling

Cars contain glass in the windows and the lights. The glass used in cars is different from that used in bottles, as it has to be strengthened for safety.

Windscreens

In the past a shattered windscreen was a common sight. Now windscreens are made from laminated glass. This is glass that is made up of two layers stuck together with a plastic glue. Laminated glass is used because it does not shatter when damaged but stays as one complete piece of glass. Windscreens often need to be repaired because the glass has been chipped by gravel and other bits flying up from the road surface.

Windscreens often have heating elements attached to the glass to melt any ice and these make recycling more difficult.

A small chip in a windscreen can usually be repaired, but large cracks are dangerous and the whole windscreen has to be replaced.

Toughened glass

The other windows in a car are made from toughened glass, which does not break as easily as a pane of glass. Sometimes these windows are tinted. Tinting is achieved by painting the glass or adding resins to the glass during its manufacture. Tinted glass is more difficult to recycle because of the colour.

Did you know...?

The average motor vehicle contains approximately 30 kg of glass – that's about 3% of the weight of a car.

Modern cars have large glass windows that give the driver good visibility. Most of the glass can be recycled, but tinted glass is more difficult. Unfortunately, cars with tinted windows are becoming more common.

Removing glass

The glass in a car is stuck in place and can be difficult to remove. Most scrapyards have to break it with a hammer, which is dangerous and often leaves bits of glass attached to the bodywork. The broken glass is put in a skip for collection by a glass recycling company. Car glass is crushed and used to make things such as glass tiles. The plastic glue in laminated glass is very expensive to buy so it is recycled. Often just the plastic from between the layers of glass in the windscreen is recycled while the glass is sent to a landfill.

Only a small percentage of glass from a car is recycled at present because of the problems of removal. Car manufacturers need to deal with these problems if more glass from cars is to be recycled in the future.

The way ahead

One way to reduce the number of cars being manufactured is to reduce the need for cars. Fewer cars on the roads mean fewer cars ending up in scrapyards.

Fewer cars in cities

There are many schemes around the world that try to persuade people to leave their cars behind and use public transport. Many of the major roads leading into cities in the USA have HOV (High Occupancy Vehicle) lanes for cars with three or more people. This encourages car sharing. In London and Singapore, vehicles entering the city centre are charged an entry fee. In London this is called congestion charging. This is to discourage people from bringing their cars into the city.

School buses help to reduce congestion, too. A bus may carry 40 or 50 pupils and avoids the need for lots of individual cars to be driven to a school.

The centre of Singapore is a restricted zone and cars have to pay money to enter it. This discourages people from driving their cars in the city centre.

Fewer resources

Large cars use more raw materials in their manufacture. So if more people bought small cars the demand for raw materials would decrease. Smaller cars weigh less and do not require so much fuel. Once a car has to be scrapped it is important that as much as possible is recycled. Currently between 75–80% of the materials (by weight) in an end-of-life vehicle are recycled in countries in the European Union and North America. This figure could be higher still.

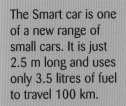

The Smart car is one of a new range of small cars. It is just 2.5 m long and uses only 3.5 litres of fuel to travel 100 km.

It's my world!

In the UK, half of all car journeys are less than 5 km. These journeys could be made on foot or by bicycle. Short car journeys are the most damaging to the environment. Catalytic converters are only effective for journeys over 5 km and the first kilometre produces 60% more fumes. Try to avoid using a car for short journeys and use a bike or go on foot instead.

Long lifespan

In the past, the life of a car was around 20 or 30 years. This was because cars were very expensive to buy and people did not replace them often. A car's lifespan is now 10–15 years. People can afford to replace cars more frequently because the cost of a new car has come down compared with earnings and often the cost of repairing an old car is more than the car is worth. Ways need to be found to encourage people to keep their cars for longer.

Glossary

Assembly line
a factory system where each worker carries out a particular job as the object (such as a car) passes by on a moving track

Battery
a device that stores electricity

Congestion
the build-up of traffic along streets

Coolant
a fluid that is used to carry heat away from something

Developed country
a country in which most people have a high standard of living

Exhaust
a system through which hot gases are allowed to escape

Fossil fuel
a fuel formed over millions of years from the remains of plants and animals, for example peat, coal, crude oil, and natural gas

Global warming
the gradual warming of the average temperature of the Earth, caused by an increase in greenhouse gases

Greenhouse gas
a gas in the atmosphere that traps heat

Landfill
a large hole in the ground that is used to dispose of waste

Ore
a type of rock that contains metal in sufficient quantity to be mined

Ozone layer
a layer high in the Earth's atmosphere that absorbs harmful ultraviolet light from the sun

Pollution
the release of harmful substances into the environment

Recycle
to process and reuse materials in order to make new items

Reduce
to lower the amount of waste that is produced

Reuse
to use something again, either in the same way or in a different way

Scrapyard
a place where end-of-life vehicles are taken to be broken up

Smog
dust, smoke and chemical fumes that pollute the air and make it hazy

Unsustainable
a level of use of a resource that cannot be maintained into the future and which will cause the resource to run out

Welding
joining metals together using heat

Websites

Cars and the Environment
www.savethekoala.com/
koalastips.html
Australian webpage giving lots of advice about how you can recycle and cut down on waste.

Car Recycling
www.wastepoint.co.uk/media/
factsheets/Cars.pdf
Webpage covering end-of-life vehicles and how they can be recycled.

End-of-Life Vehicle and Tyre Recycling
www.wasteonline.org.uk/resources/
InformationSheets/vehicle.htm
Webpage with lots of details about end-of-life vehicles in the UK.

Friends of the Earth
www.foe.org.uk
Website of the charity Friends of the Earth that gives information about campaigns, including those for encouraging recycling and against incinerators and landfills.

Plastics and Cars
www.plastics-car.com/s_plasticscar/
doc.asp?CID=407&DID=1608
Webpage giving information about the use of plastics in cars and how they are recycled.

Recycle Now: Tyre Recycling
www.recyclenow.com/at_leisure/
tyre_recycling.html
Part of a useful website on all aspects of recycling, this webpage discusses the life of a recycled tyre.

US Environmental Protection Agency
www.epa.gov
This website has lots of environmental information on all issues, not just waste. There is an EPA Kids Club (www.epa.gov/kids) with information on waste and recycling.

US Environmental Protection Agency: Batteries
This page gives information about batteries:
www.epa.gov/epaoswer/non-hw/
muncpl/battery.htm

Every effort has been made by the Publisher to ensure that these websites are suitable for children and contain no inappropriate or offensive material. However, because of the nature of the internet it is impossible to guarantee that the contents of these sites will not be altered. We strongly advise that internet access is supervised by a responsible adult.

Index